Praise For SOTH

"Survival of the Hive utilizes the roles of bees in the hive to show us the value of Servant leadership in guiding an organization to meet its goals. We also realize how much the leader "communicates" without saying a word and how important it is to listen for the buzz! Kudos to Deborah and Matt for sharing the lessons of the hive!"
—Michele Kelly, Chief Financial Officer, Catholic Charities

"I have read hundreds of business leadership books and still found this book timely, interesting, and easily adaptable to share with teams. The chapters for each skill are short, to the point, and include a chapter ending list of questions to provoke conversation and understanding. This book is a great tool to develop leadership in teams!"
—Jared Eckler, President, Townsend Leather Company

"Creative and fun way to educate seasoned as well as new managers on the importance of leading your team to success!"
—Liz Fisher, Human Resources Manager, Boise Paper

"In addition to being a good read, The Survival of the Hive is an effective business tool. Mackin and Harrington take the timeless concepts of strategy, vision, belief and purpose and translate them into a multi-dimensional package full of ideas to help enhance your corporate culture. The Honeycomb Model blended with the 4R Strategy, Perfect Product, CAMP, Front Porch and many other approaches provide great topics for conversation and are bound to elicit creative new ideas for managers and the teams they lead. Once again, Mackin and Harrington use their vast experience in transforming teams and corporate cultures to help leaders evolve on the path to success!"
—Melissa Feck, Vice President of Human Resources,
Healthcare Association of New York State

Survival of the Hive

7 Leadership Lessons From a Beehive

Deborah Mackin
and
Matthew Harrington

authorHOUSE®

AuthorHouse™
1663 Liberty Drive
Bloomington, IN 47403
www.authorhouse.com
Phone: 1-800-839-8640

Published by AuthorHouse 5/14/2013

ISBN: 978-1-4817-4972-5 (sc)
ISBN: 978-1-4817-4971-8 (hc)
ISBN: 978-1-4817-4970-1 (e)

Library of Congress Control Number: 2013908670

Dedication

Deborah Mackin: To my husband and co-beekeeper, Paul Mackin, who readily encouraged the development of the book and read and edited endlessly; to my sons, Michael and Matt Harrington, my stepchildren and grandchildren, with a special note to Matt, for the sheer joy of writing together and our time on Cape Cod; and to our bee mentors, Mel and John Letourneau.

Matthew Harrington: To my seventh grade English teacher, Emilie Bastian, who gave me the spark and interest to develop the craft of writing and the confidence to do something with it. To my mother, without whom none of this would be possible—you are my mentor, my inspiration, and my friend. To many more trips to the Cape!

Table of Contents

Acknowledgments

Bee Book references: The following books were used to fact check our information on bees and beekeeping.

- ▶ *Storey's Guide to Keeping Honey Bees*, Malcolm Sanford and Richard Bonney, Storey Publishing, 2010
- ▶ *The Backyard Beekeeper*, Kim Flottum, Quarry Books, 2010
- ▶ *The New Complete Guide to Beekeeping*, Roger A. Morse, Countrymen Press, 1994

Our readers: Those readers who helped in the development of the story line and flow of the book: Paul Mackin, Sarah Imboden, Laura Dehmer, Judy Pennock, Lisa Dunbar, Berta Winiker and endorsers of the book.

Our leader friends: To all the leaders we have coached and trained over the years who demonstrate characteristics of positive leadership, so important and valued in their organization.

Our illustrator: To Paul Miraglia, who helped build a great creative concept around the bee culture and the business world—not an easy feat! Your creativeness, humor, and most importantly, willingness and excitement around the project have been such an encouragement to us. We hope this is the start to a great career for you.

A special thanks to Dan and Lauren Gulotti of Madlab Design for a terrific cover design, website and for many renditions of each.

Week after week the hive is transformed, helping us to see valuable leadership lessons in their activity

Introduction

When we purchased our first beehive, after carefully placing the queen in the hive, we tipped the box upside down and shook 5,000 bees into the hive. At first the bees were flying everywhere. But within minutes all the bees had settled into the hive and begun their work.

During the past three years as beekeepers, it's been remarkable to open the hive and see the "industry" of honey making evolve through the various seasons of the year. In the spring, the hive has the fewest number of bees, and the scramble is on to build up the bee population and start honey production again. By summertime, the hive is in full production as the bee count dramatically increases and the honey cells are filled and capped. In the fall, the bees should have all the honey they need for the winter—the drones are gone, and the hive is sealed from the cold.

When you take the lid off the hive and watch the bees for any length of time, you will soon see the culture of the beehive. Every bee is industrious and purposeful. Communication occurs among the bees quickly. The queen is hard at work populating the hive and moving over the cells to ensure all the work of survival gets accomplished. Week after week the hive is transformed, helping us to see valuable leadership lessons in all their activity.

The chapters of this book include both the macro- and micro-responsibilities of a queen bee and her relationship to a hive. Each chapter explores how the beehive functions through the characters of Zync, a queen-in-waiting, and her fellow bees. Using the bee colony as an allegory to illustrate leadership in an organized community, we provide a working illustration of cultural complexity, leadership clarity, and the importance of trust as a foundation for excellence.

Although one might assume a queen bee represents a female style of leadership, the leadership lessons within the book are not gender specific. We encourage every reader to look past gender and focus on the key lessons applicable to all. We have also included a number of illustrations throughout the book to lend it levity and curiosity for the reader.

The Mid-Atlantic Agriculture Research and Extension Consortium describe the bee colony and its organization this way:

> Honey bees are social insects, which mean that they live together in large, well-organized family groups. Social insects are highly evolved insects that engage in a variety of complex tasks not practiced by the multitude of solitary insects. Communication, complex nest construction, environmental control, defense, and division of the labor are just some of the behaviors that honey bees have developed to exist successfully in social colonies. These fascinating behaviors make social insects in general, and honey bees in particular, among the most fascinating creatures on earth. ("The Colony and Its Organization," Mid-Atlantic Apiculture Research and Extension Consortium, 7 August 2012)

We have taken some license in the use of the beehive analogy to illustrate key beehive lessons we feel are important for today's leaders in organizations and businesses. As we bring the hive to life through the personification of the various bees within the hive, our apologies to beekeepers, who may chuckle at the characters we've created. We have, however, been true to the specific activities of the hive—whether the dancing, the pheromone system, or the cooperativeness of the bee culture. Interestingly, it takes 300 bees visiting two million flowers and flying over 55,000 miles to make one pound of honey. That one pound of honey is the only food that includes all the substances necessary to sustain life, including water.

While many of the leadership traits we discuss are actually instinctual to bees, for the purpose of illustration we have added human tendencies to the bees to bring these traits to life. We then take those leadership lessons, at the conclusion of each chapter, and reflect on leadership within organizations. These reflections include examples of how the beehive traits can help today's leaders achieve better outcomes. What does it mean to be focused on survival? How does a community expand and contract dramatically and not dissolve into chaos?

At the end of each chapter we have included key questions for leadership groups to discuss and develop on their own. These discussions will especially help new, emerging leaders recognize and embrace the importance of the seven leadership lessons. We encourage discussion facilitators to demonstrate the same principles within the book in order to encourage transparent discussions of issues and different perspectives.

You mold your leadership style to what is best for the hive, not what draws attention to you.

1. Survival of the Hive

"**G**et ready, Zync, get ready! They may swarm at any moment. It's too crowded in the hive, and the queen has told us she's planning to take flight!"

Hanging upside down at the bottom of the bee frame in a queen cell, Zync pleaded, "But I'm not ready to be a queen bee yet. I know the beehive philosophy is unique, but no one has taught me how to be the leader of the hive. Tell her she can't leave yet!"

Earlier that day, the queen had summoned three veteran bees, Vision, Strategy, and Belief, to prepare Zync, the queen-in-waiting, for her inevitable role. Vision and Strategy will teach Zync the leadership approach in a beehive culture, while Belief will challenge and correct Zync's assumptions about leadership.

Her three mentors will have to work quickly to get her ready before the existing queen takes flight, an inescapable fact of every hive when it becomes overcrowded or reproduction of colonies is needed. The queen takes half the hive with her, leaving behind the honey, the brood (un-hatched bee larvae) and half of the bees in the hive for Zync, as the new queen. While Zync is in her queen cell, the bees that will leave are consuming honey for the journey and sorting who will stay and who will go, as the scout bees go out in advance looking for a new home.

Zync's first job as queen will be to take her maiden flight with a dozen or so drones and then populate the hive with enough bees to make sufficient honey for the upcoming winter months.

1

Unity of Purpose: Survival of the Hive

"There is nothing more important for you as a leader than the *survival of the hive*." Strategy begins to teach Zync. "You must be single-minded in this purpose, Zync. This is not about the bee culture molding to your leadership preferences but about your leadership molding to the purpose and culture of the hive."

"I know that may sound strange, Zync, as many leaders have their own style of leadership and expect everyone to adapt to them. But in the beehive culture, you mold your leadership style to what is best for the hive, not what draws attention to you or fits your personality preference," Vision added.

Strategy and Vision have been teaching the queen bees for years that leadership isn't about having a big hive with many frames or about demanding all the attention and respect. Being the leader is knowing how to keep the hive alive, responding to the environment outside the hive, and storing enough honey to sustain the hive during the cold, barren months when no food or resources are available. Growth in the hive and attention for the leader will occur naturally as the hive thrives.

Times of Change

"There will be times of plenty and times of hardship for the hive," Belief admonished, "and as queen you must prepare us for both. The more resources we are able to produce efficiently to gather pollen and nectar for honey production, the greater the success of the hive.

"As the leader, your most important function is to sustain the hive," Belief continued matter-of-factly. "If you can't do that, we will have to find a new queen who can. You are leader as long as you fulfill the *survival of the hive* priority—what is best for our community as a whole."

Zync listened attentively to the leadership points being made by Strategy, Vision, and Belief. "That sounds like I have to be always

Today's leaders can become confused about what is most important: their own survival or the organization's survival.

thinking of the good of the hive, not just what's good for me as queen, right?"

"There may be times when you are tempted to focus on yourself and your needs, but that is not good leadership, Zync," Belief stressed. "We all have to work hard to overcome the tendency to believe that we—meaning any one of us—are more important than the whole hive."

Strategy continued, "A leader must commit to the total good of the hive first. There are many tasks that must get done, but every one of those tasks is aligned to our survival, not just to you."

"Like what tasks?" Zync questioned, wanting a better understanding of the details around survival.

"Right now you are in your queen cell sac, Zync, and can't see all the activity that's going on in the hive. Once you are out of the sac, you will see that as the leader, you must ensure that the hive has an adequate supply of resources to go get and produce the food that will keep everyone alive," Strategy explained.

"You must help us commit to our shared value of community, working together, storing the honey properly and communicating with us so we all know what's best every day. We must believe you care more about the hive than you care about yourself," Strategy finished.

Survival of the Hive: Reflections for Today's Leaders

Every bee in the hive understands the significance of keeping the colony alive and healthy as a way to ensure their future. They are not confused about their number one priority. As the new leader, Zync must understand that her priority is to the *survival of the hive*, which in her case means producing the resources needed and keeping her hive together in community. Leaders today can often become misguided about their ultimate purpose. With pressure from various stakeholders and constantly changing environments, today's leaders can become confused about what is most important: their own survival or the organization's survival. During difficult or stressful times, it's natural to the focus on oneself for preservation and miss the importance of the larger mission of a leader.

Survival of the Hive Mentality

Zync is guided by Vision, Strategy, and Belief in the formation of her leadership style. Today's leaders need this same mentoring and guidance to define the vision, strategy, purpose, beliefs, and values for their own organizations, departments, or teams. We see Zync being carefully taught to focus her ambition on the good of the hive and to think proactively rather than reactively. Ambition and power are seductive to leaders and can draw the focus away from the good of the organization or department. When this happens, leaders become more attracted to a short-term, reactive approach that offers immediate gratification than to working toward the long-term, proactive needs of the organization, team, or department. We are demonstrating a proactive, *survival of the hive* mentality when we ask questions like these:

► What is best right now for my organization, department or team, regardless of its impact on me?
► Are our vision and strategy clear and unified?
► Do our beliefs or values and behaviors align with our vision and strategy?
► Am I, as a leader, helping to secure the necessary resources for our survival?
► As we adapt to change, are we maintaining our focus on the right things?

Equally, leaders must be self-sacrificing, not self-serving, and devoted to their hive with a bold strategy to see it succeed. This important shift in focus from being obsessed about self-survival to having an unrelenting passion to see a whole organization thrive

5

is vital for leadership. This philosophy shifts a leader from placing importance solely on his/her own "silo," or pet project, to a larger objective focused on the survival of the whole organization.

Your followers will sense if your agenda is self-serving or if it is focused on what is needed for everyone. Sometimes, this may put a leader in the difficult position of having to tell others what isn't working right or how things need to change. Sometimes it's having courage to say what is unpopular or different from what other leaders are saying. If the intention is for the survival of the whole, you'll know it's the right thing to do.

The most important question for a leader to be asking at every turn is this: *How is what I'm doing ensuring the survival of the organization long term?* Every restructuring, merger, acquisition, consolidation, reorganization, and/or transformation must address this question first. The link between every decision and survival must be clearly seen by all. The primary focus must be on the organization, not the extension of one's leadership term, not even the expansion of one's department or project.

Leadership Readiness

We see Zync is not ready to be a leader yet, even though she has to become one very quickly. Many leaders are promoted into leadership without the proper preparation to achieve success. In our story, we see the queen bee calling Vision, Strategy, and Belief to prepare Zync for her leadership role before the queen takes flight. She knows that the hive must not fall apart when she leaves. The legacy for this queen is leaving the best leadership behind for the hive. It's good to remind leaders today that what occurs after they leave is a testimony to the quality of their leadership while they were in the organization. The best test of someone's leadership is to look at the department or team after they've left to see if it falls apart and loses focus without the ever-present leader pushing things forward.

No organization or department should be built for the leader but rather to ensure that the organization or department survives and even thrives past any single leader. The leader must ask, "How well am I preparing my 'hive' to survive past my leadership?"

Group Discussion Questions

1. What does *survival of the hive* mean for our organization? Is it clearly our number-one priority? As a leadership entity, have we broken away from silo thinking and united around a single purpose, common vision, and joint objectives?
2. As leaders within our organization or department, is our focus on building a strong hive, rather than demonstrating our own strength? Is our message confusing to the other "bees in our hive"? Does the staff feel we have a personal agenda that is the real reason for our actions?
3. How are we preparing our next leaders for the roles they will need to assume when we "take flight"?
4. How are our new leaders being mentored and trained in the expectations we have for them as leaders and in the vision and beliefs of the organization so that they continue what has been built before them?
5. If we find ourselves off course, what can we do as leaders today to get back to a *survival of the hive* approach?

2. The P-Factors of Leadership

"**Z**ync, because you have been chosen to be the next queen, you have been endowed with what we call Queen Substance, or the *P-Factors* of Leadership. This is a leadership essence, an ability through proper training and practice that you can call upon and use to direct the *survival of the hive*. Your P-Factors will cause great changes in the behavior of other bees. They must never be used for self-gain or aggrandizement but rather for the good of the hive. With the talent of the *P-Factors* comes great responsibility to use them effectively," Vision said.

A Complex P-Factor System

"We bees have one of the most complex pheromone systems found in nature, what we call our *P-Factors* for short. We possess glands that produce an array of offensive and defensive signals for the hive. You have four key leadership *P-Factors* that make you special as our leader: the *Footprint, Resourcing, Calming,* and *Unity P-Factors.* Wise use of your *P-Factors* will build our sense of community and commitment and determine the hive's success," Strategy said.

"As bees, we also have a *P-Factor*—the *Alarms*—that works with you for the good of the hive," Belief added.

"Let's discuss each of these factors," Strategy continued. "Each

9

factor can work alone, but together they build an all-inclusive commitment within the hive to follow your leadership. Let's look at each one individually. Be sure to ask questions as we go along."

The Footprint P-Factor

"Let's begin with the *Footprint P-Factor*. As you walk around over the cells of the hive, you secrete a *Footprint P-Factor* that lets the other bees know your presence has been there," Belief said. "It is your presence that builds trust within the hive as you lead by example. Other bees will share the stories of your footprint everywhere they go, building upon your leadership presence. If you fail to show your leadership footprint, if you are not out among on us, you will frighten the hive, because they will wonder whether you exist and whether you care and understand what they're experiencing."

"As queen you must never distance yourself from the other bees in the hive by isolating yourself or preferring a small group of bees over others. A leadership footprint like that will build distrust and division within the hive," Vision added.

Building Followership

"For those bees who work outside the hive, they must know that you trust them to do excellent work. Your *Footprint P-Factor* will build their followership, as they desire to submit to your leadership. They must have pride in who you are and what you stand for as a leader in order for them to want to find their way back home. It is stressful for our forager bees to be out of the hive, sometimes flying far away to gather the pollen and nectar. When they return they must sense that all is well within the hive," Vision concluded.

"Zync, leadership is about being present and approachable. How frequently do you move about the hive? How aware are you of the tone and mood of your hive? Your *Footprint P-Factor* will show that

It is your presence that builds trust within the hive, as you lead by example. Other bees will share the stories of your footprint everywhere they go, building upon your leadership presence.

you are present and accept the responsibility of leadership," Belief said soberly.

"That makes sense," Zync replied, "I will leave the footprint of a strong, active, and present queen."

The Resourcing P-Factor

"Under your direction, the correct amount of resources required for the hive are identified, created, and appropriately assigned," Strategy instructed, "and those that are detrimental or unimportant are removed. You have the capacity within you to determine the number and types of bees needed. We depend on your judgment here, Zync, so plan wisely. Then you will instruct the nurse bees to help the resources that are good for the hive to grow and those that are not to be removed, based on your *Resourcing P-Factor*."

"Remember, if you under-resource the hive by producing an insufficient number of bees, the hive will die for lack of honey in the barren months. It might be tempting to skimp on resources for short-term gain, but it will work against you in the long run. As the leader, you must think of the long-term good of the hive, not only what makes sense or is convenient for the short term," Vision added.

"But how will I know what the hive will need in the long term?"

"Very good question, Zync, and one that confuses many leaders," Belief said. "It is your job as queen to assess the risks associated with every season of the hive, not just to react to the urge of the moment. We'll discuss this more as we go along, as signaling risk to the hive is a critical part of all our jobs."

The Alarm P-Factor

"Now that we're discussing risk," Vision said, lowering her voice so other bees couldn't hear and get upset, "we want you to know that there are two *Alarm P-Factors* every bee is equipped with, but we must be careful not to set off any alarms as we talk.

"One is the highly volatile, *Attack Alarm* (our A-Alarm), and the other is the cautious, assertive *Repel Alarm* (our R-Alarm). The bees must know when to set off the A-Alarm when outsiders attack and when to use the R-Alarm to repel those risks that are less dangerous and simply need to be contained or restrained."

"Wait, wait. I'm confused," Zync countered. "How are they different?"

"The *Attack-Alarm* is our most powerful signal to all the bees in the colony," Strategy said. "It instructs them that we are under attack and they must sting the enemy. We use our stingers only when the A-Alarm sounds because we each have only one stinger and when we lose it we make the ultimate sacrifice for the hive. So we must be very careful not to signal an A-alarm unless absolutely necessary. That's why Vision was whispering."

"Ultimate sacrifice? Are you saying we ... die?" Zync exclaimed.

"Regardless of what we are doing," Belief continued, "we must stop and help the guard bees, so they aren't overwhelmed or outnumbered. It might be a bear or a human who wants our honey; we must all respond to the danger and work together to protect the hive from the aggressor."

Vision added, "Other times we use the Repel-Alarm to repel the possibility of an attack. We might be visited by robber bees or a mouse that want to steal what we have or potential enemies of the hive who want to take over. We repel these attacks by joining together as a team and escorting the attacker out of the hive by the arms and legs or covering it with propolis, our waxy seal, so it can't move. We handle these attacks without losing our stingers, making our Repel-Alarm a much more resource-conscious alarm."

"I see. We all are responsible for raising our level of awareness and urgency and making it known to the entire hive so we respond correctly. Sometimes that will mean attack and other times that will mean repel, right?"

Vision smiled. "She's a smart one."

We must be transparent and clear and never, ever suggest false threats just to get the hive to work harder.

"Yes," Belief said, "our job is to communicate the level of threats to the hive. Is this an A-Alarm threat or a R-Alarm threat? Does this require all of our resources or just some of them? We must be transparent and clear, and never, ever suggest false threats just to get the hive to work harder or to 'pull together for the sake of the hive.'"

The Calming P-Factor

"This is hard. There's so much to remember and my leadership is so important. What if I make mistakes and the bees don't follow me? What if I forget to move around and leave my footprint?"

"You're anxious, Zync, but it's because we haven't given you the *Calming P-Factor* yet. All you can think of right now are all the 'what ifs' that might occur, and that can make you frantic as a leader," Strategy concurred.

"Every queen must be a calming influence on the hive, especially when there's change or fear among the bees. Although you may feel scared, hungry, or cold, you must never show the other bees that you are scared, hungry, or cold, because if you show these feelings, your colony will act the same. You must be a steady, consistent presence during the many seasons of your leadership," Vision said.

"The *Calming P-Factor* is one of your most important attributes as a leader," Belief added. "You will need it for the short term when the bees come to you and anxiously want an answer. You will also use this factor for the long term to sustain the social behavior of the hive when swarming occurs and during the reproductive process, when you leave the hive temporarily without a queen. Everything we do as a hive must have your calming influence, or we will be misguided and anxious about everything. You must help us pick those things that require our focus and remind us that we can't always control everything. As part of nature, we are responsible for the effort, not the end result, which is really determined by a multitude of factors that are outside our control."

"Especially when the population in the hive increases and we're very busy and getting in each other's way. Any change will cause the bees to be anxious. Your *Calming P-Factor* helps us focus and maintain a spirit of cooperation during change," Belief added.

Zync smiled. "I think I sense it right now. I'm not as anxious as I was just a moment ago."

The Retinue or Unity P-Factor

"What does retinue mean?" Zync questioned.

"The retinue is your ability to form a cohesive culture and comradeship within the hive," Belief said.

"Phew, that's hard to remember and say!" Zync said, looking discouraged.

The three bees laughed. "That's what the other queens used to say. We've come to call it simply the *Unity P-Factor*. It is our team culture, our values, and our willingness to follow and support each other," Vision said.

Following the Leader

Strategy added, "You need to ask yourself: do the bees follow me, or do they resist? What do I attract around me as leader of the hive? Am I a queen that promotes unity of purpose, excellence and teamwork? Or, am I a queen who tolerates conflict, favoritism, and strife? You see, the *Unity P-Factor* is at the heart of the culture you've created within the hive."

"Equally, your leadership must reinforce the correct boundaries for rebellious bees, correcting behavior that doesn't align with our *survival of the hive* approach," Vision added.

"In the end, the *survival of the hive* is not only about the strength of you but the strength and culture of all those who follow you. What culture have you created? What kind of hive have you formed? What behavior do you encourage or allow," Vision said.

The best leaders lead out of a place of promise,
not out of fear.

Belief added with emphasis, "Bottom line, the question is: Can the bees trust you and be honest without fear of your anger and wrath? The best leaders lead out of a place of promise, not out of fear. And it is because of this place of promise that your message is communicated and distributed effectively throughout the ranks to every member of the hive. We want to share your message with each other because we believe it. The more you exude this *Unity P-Factor*, the more your spirit, your movement, your sound will send a message to the rest of the hive. Other bees sense this *Unity P-Factor* and respond to your leadership."

The P-Factor Reflections for Today's Leaders

The pheromone system in the queen bee automatically ensures that her leadership provides a sense of her presence (footprint), an adequate number of bees (resourcing), assurance to the hive (calming) and common purpose and community (unity). Interestingly, the queen relies on the other bees to set off the alarm pheromones.

When we think about it, all leaders have certain essences or P-Factor attributes that influence an organization, department, or team's success to a profound effect. Whether the leader is the head of the organization, or a departmental or section leader, these attributes—or the lack of them—influence the entire culture of the organization.

Leaving a Footprint

Zync is first instructed that her footprint leaves an impression wherever she goes; the same is true for every leader. What footprint does the leader make? Is the footprint limited to only periodic sightings when things go wrong? Strong leaders leave a positive, strong footprint as they move throughout the organization—a conversation here or there, a note of praise near a metric board, a "from the desk of ..." communication that updates the organization. The leader's footprint can be large or small, positive or negative. Based on this footprint, people decide whether to follow the leader or actively resist. What is the nature of your footprint? How far and deep does it go in your organization?

As an example, leaders often fail to communicate enough when change is occurring in the organization. They neglect to schedule visits to departments and teams to explain the case for the change and the vision for the future. This lack of a "footprint" leaves people stressed about the change, imagining the worst and susceptible to the negative projections of resistors.

Securing the Resources Needed to Succeed

Zync is responsible as the queen for resourcing her hive with enough bees to produce the honey that is needed. She is single-minded in her effort, laying sometimes 2,000 eggs per day. Our question to leaders is: Are you providing adequate resources to get the work done, or are you always suggesting that people need to do more with less? There is a breaking point where under-resourcing can place your department, team, or organization at great risk. Conversely, paying too little attention to a ballooning resource pool will cause over-expenditures. Careful resource planning is an imperative of a good leader.

During tough economic times when organizations are tempted to "cut to the bone" on resources, there needs to be conversation about the longer-term impact of those decisions and the risks associated. Are we leaving ourselves open to quality risks? Are we overtaxing our high performers to the point where they will want to leave?

Sounding the Alarms

The leader must also be wise about what alarms are communicated throughout the group or organization. If everything sets off an alarm, then soon no one is listening. And, interestingly as the beehive illustrates, there are offensive and defensive alarms. Sometimes it's necessary to attack and sometimes it's necessary to be able to defend or repel the attack. As a leader, are attacks focused outside the hive, or are employees allowed to attack within the hive? Notice that bees never attack each other, only those threats outside the hive. They are also very careful about how many resources they use to respond to a threat or an attack.

Calming the Fears

In today's world of constant change, the *Calming P-Factor* may be one of the most important for leaders. Running around like "Chicken Little" only creates anxiety and confusion. In the most turbulent and chaotic times, it is the best leaders that keep a steady hand, focus their vision on the horizon, and exude confidence in themselves as well as their hive.

Unity of Purpose

And finally, the retinue, or *Unity P-Factor*, that builds unity of purpose, a culture of excellence and community so clear and vital that no one can mistake it, is not about being the most feared leader or the most commanding one but rather the leader that can unify the organization, team, or department around a sense of purpose and galvanize it to action in a positive way.

Effective leaders leave a footprint, resource correctly, calm others, and unite people around a common purpose. They recognize that alarms are often set off by others and toward others, even within the organization, department, or team. A strong leader reminds people to respond only to alarms that represent real and present danger to the *survival of the hive.*

Group Discussion Questions

1. How does our leadership at various levels within the organization demonstrate the vital *P-Factors of Leadership* as illustrated in the beehive story?

    a. **The Footprint P-Factor**: moving throughout the hive so frequently that the leader's visits are seen as normal. What is the size, tone, and frequency of our leadership footprints?

    b. **The Resourcing P-Factor**: ensuring that the department, team, or organization has adequate resources to do its work and is never short-changed. In times of economic turmoil are we squeezing the resources too tightly without modifying expectations?

    c. **The Alarm P-Factor**: clearly signaling attacks from the outside and knowing when to respond defensively from the inside. If, as leaders, we realize that the Attack-Alarm will ultimately kill us (as we lose our stingers), would we be more mindful of when the A-Alarm is sounded? Equally, do we have a good defensive strategy when the situation calls for it? Do we work together, like the bees, to repel or eliminate the threat?

    d. **The Calming P-Factor**: demonstrating such a calming demeanor that anxiety and fear are reduced and contained and the hive is able to focus on what's critical to do. Would we be described as possessing the *Calming P-Factor* essence in our leadership approach?

    e. **The Unity P-Factor**: developing a sense of unity, teamwork, and collaboration within the organization, department, or team. Consider how a beehive grows in just three to four months—from less than a thousand bees to more than 50,000 bees—while never losing its unity of purpose. Are we consciously building a unity culture every single day? How are we doing this?

3. The Colony Culture

"**O**f course, Zync, the hive wouldn't succeed if not for all the other bees that play different and vital roles in the development of the hive. I'm sure you've realized that as queen bee you do not make pollen into honey. Nor do you fan the hive or nurse the brood. You don't go out and scout or forage, nor do you bring water to cool the hive during the hot summer months. The other bees are the number one resource in your hive," Strategy said.

Keeping the Beehive Alive

"We all work together for a collective purpose, for keeping the beehive alive!" Zync said.

"Yes, the hive as a whole is more important to every bee than their individual work of capping, foraging, or cleaning. We are very careful not to build divisions between the work done in our hive, so no bees are more interested in their own work than in the work of the whole hive," Strategy said.

"You see, it's not only the colony that should concern you, but each individual bee too," Belief chimed in. "Every bee has a specific purpose and reason for being here. They each have tasks to accomplish, but they need your direction and guidance throughout their existence in the hive. It is your role to communicate to the whole of the hive *and* to reach out to each bee as an important link to the hive's success. There are so many of us that it's easy for each bee to think she or he doesn't matter, or that others will do the work. They must believe that what they do is important and vital to our survival. They will if you, as the leader, help them to see why they are significant contributors to our colony. If you believe in them, they will believe in themselves, and our colony culture will thrive.

"I've got it. I've got it. I'll go out and meet with each and every bee when I first become the queen and tell them how important they are to the hive."

"Wait just a minute, Zync," Belief said. "It's not about just meeting every bee when you first become queen. It's not about showing off or creating the appearance of caring. What would be your commitment to do it a second or third or fourth time? This is not about your image as queen. If you truly care, you will know when it's important to be out among the bees, listening to their concerns and their successes and encouraging and recognizing their effort. It's about identifying with the bees in your hive, Zync, and making a strong connection with them."

Understanding How We Function

"Let's step back for a moment, mentors," Belief suggested. "I think Zync needs to understand better how the hive functions."

"I agree," Strategy said. "You see, when a bee is born, it first works within the hive—or house as we sometimes call it—to learn how the hive functions. There are many jobs it must learn to perform: building and cleaning the honey and brood cells within the frame, bringing you special food as the queen, sealing the hive with propolis to keep out the wind, fanning the hive to cool it down, covering the honey cells with wax, and protecting and nursing the brood to life. Each worker bee must perform the assigned task but also be flexible to learn new tasks. You will rarely see a single bee cap a honey cell by itself. Instead, you'll see a team of bees cap the cell as they happen to come across

We are careful not to build divisions
between the work done in our hive,
so no bees are more interested in their
own work than in the work of the whole hive.

it and decide together that something needs to be done about it. We are a *colony culture* that believes in teamwork. Each member must be prepared to do whatever is necessary for the good of the whole."

Flexing Our Roles to the Need at Hand

"The worker bees' adaptability to change from one task to another with a few seconds' notice seems remarkable," Zync noted.

Vision nodded and added, "Once the worker bees mature, they move outside the hive and are assigned the roles of scout or forager. These are very difficult roles because the bees must leave the hive and its protection to go out into the world—as far away from the hive as needed—to find and gather the pollen and nectar to make the honey. The wind tears at their wings and they are vulnerable to attack by predators."

"You may think," Belief added, "that being away from the hive is exciting or exotic; however, to the contrary, a bee away from the hive for a significant amount of time experiences great stress and feels weak and disconnected. When it returns to the hive, it will need time to be refreshed and restored by the bee community before going away again."

"It's neat to think how much we need each other and our *colony culture* for continuous support and encouragement," Zync added.

Vision agreed. "You'll see that we greet and help every scout and forager bee as they come back so they know how important they are to the hive. Don't underestimate the importance of greeting and engaging your traveling bees. As leader, you are the initiator, the one responsible for reaching out to all of us."

"Now, let's discuss the role of drones," Strategy said. "The drone's role is limited in the colony. Drones lack stingers, so they cannot help defend the hive. Without any way to collect pollen or nectar, they cannot contribute to feeding the community. Yet they are important to us because they will mate with you after you leave the queen cell. These drones will accompany you on your maiden flight. We always have a significant number of drones in the hive in the event that we need to create a new queen, just like we are doing with you now. Even though the role is limited, we treat them with great respect and value their contribution."

"There's another interesting thing to note about our hive," Vision added. "There is never a time when the whole colony sleeps. While some bees take time to rest and restore, others bees continue to work so the hive is never inactive. If there is work to be done, the hive gets it done. It is a constant buzzing of productivity and good work ethic!"

"We have an amazing colony culture, don't we? And there's a reason and method to everything we do," Zync said proudly.

The Importance of "We"

Belief spoke next. "The beehive and all that we can accomplish in a season is very impressive, but it is the 'we' factor that makes it possible. You'll notice you have no wax glands, your stinger is lightly barbed and curved, and you have no pollen baskets on your hind legs. You cannot do all the roles that the hive requires to survive. Even though you are queen, you are dependent on the abilities of the others no matter how small, young or old they may seem. Every role serves a purpose and no role is greater than any other."

"In that vein, Zync, you may get the urge to tell others bees what to do and how to do it because you are queen, but they know best how to accomplish their work. It is our recommendation that you do not interfere with the work that is being done within your hive," Vision said.

"I'm confused again," Zync said. "I thought it was my role to communicate all that I wanted to have done within the hive through my P-Factors? I mean, I am the queen!"

A Relationship of Trust

"This is correct," said Strategy. "However, here's the difference. Your role is to build the *colony culture* and provide direction and reason to the colony. But you must also trust your bees to do the work they know how to do. You send out the '*what* needs to be done' and '*why* it needs to get done' messages. They determine the '*how* it will be done.' It is a great relationship of trust between the queen and her followers. It is a relationship built upon transparency, reliance on one another and an unwavering commitment to the common goal to see the hive survive."

The Honeycomb Model

"One way to remember our interconnectedness and unity of purpose, Zync," Belief added, "is to look at the way the honeycomb in our hive is formed. The hexagon design causes the cell wall of one cell to become the wall of another cell. All the cells are linked together to strengthen the total frame that holds the weight of our honey."

"There are no empty spaces; there are no cracks, gaps or divides in our honeycomb. We are all bound together," Strategy concluded.

The Colony Culture Reflection for Today's Leaders

Instinctually the bees know the value of being in colony with each other. And they experience the stress, just as we do, when they try to go it alone. The walls of the honey comb are a powerful symbol of this connection of one to another. Are you 'in colony' within your organization, department, or team? Do your interactions look like a honeycomb?

Shared Roles and Responsibilities

The bees move fluidly from one role to another, working in pairs or small groups to get the job done. Zync is reminded that the bees know best how to do their work and don't need her telling them what to do. So often we hear leaders today say, "Why are they doing it that way? They should do it this way!" They engage in micromanaging and failing to delegate rather than asking what the individual or team thinks is best and letting them do it. Leaders are disempowering their workers when they deliver the "how" with the "what and the why," discouraging staff from figuring it out themselves.

Sometimes the complexity of the organizational structure, or even global responsibilities, can create considerable distance between the leader and the workforce. The leader is often far removed from the actual work being done. It can be easy to assume that a process can happen more quickly, with fewer resources, or that bottlenecks and constraints are caused by people rather than broken systems. Great leaders use their *Footprint P-Factor* and go to where the action is and ask the worker to explain the process and what needs to improve. They respect the roles of each and delegate effectively to others.

Sometimes leaders can have the right idea but execute the idea in a less than desirable way. Zync suggests that she'll meet each bee in the beginning but is quickly admonished by Belief not to do actions for appearance's sake but rather to demonstrate that she truly cares about the bees. Here again the *Footprint P-Factor* constantly reinforces the importance of being present as a leader in the hive. Many people in organizations develop loyalties with those with whom they work closely but lack a real commitment to leadership and the organization as a whole. The leader's *Unity P-Factor* can provide a constant reminder that we are one organization with one purpose.

A Flexible, Dynamic Work System

The beehive work system is extremely flexible and dynamic based on the needs of the hive. Teamwork is the norm and role shifting is constant. It's fascinating to realize that the bees keep new bees within the hive, close to the queen, learning how the hive functions and doing basic tasks. Later, as the bees mature, they are assigned the more isolated and difficult tasks of scouting and foraging. This approach might be interesting for leaders to consider: keeping new employees close to the leadership to build an understanding of the culture, philosophy, and approach before they are assigned more difficult or lonely tasks.

Providing Resources and Support

Another interesting insight from the colony culture is the recognition that bees that travel away from the hive experience stress and need encouragement and support when they return to the community. Many global organizations have employees working in different countries or traveling constantly and don't necessarily recognize the toll on their work and personal lives. Dealing with cross-cultural differences can impact the sense of unity toward the whole. Providing time and resources to rejuvenate and refresh leaders may be very important, especially for those who travel frequently.

Most importantly, organizational leaders must recognize that they need to allow the workforce to do their work. The temptation to try to do it all, or to tell others how to do their jobs, will be a misguided use of their time. The leader provides direction by defining the "what and the why" for the workforce, team, or department. They begin with the "why," explaining why we are here and why we might need to change. Then the leader defines the "what" by encouraging a particular target or goal. The best leaders ask workers to participate in the development of the "how." If more leaders could remember this approach, workers would feel more engaged, trusted, and responsible for their contribution.

Zync recognizes as the leader that she sets the tone for a *colony culture* of teamwork, shared roles and responsibilities, and commitment to a strong work ethic and common purpose. She provides direction and trusts that others are equally capable of performing the tasks that need to get done. She supports the uniqueness of her role and the uniqueness of every other role in the hive.

The leader provides direction by defining the 'what' and the 'why' for the workforce, team or department. It is the job of the other bees to determine the 'how.'

Group Discussion Questions

1. This chapter speaks to being "in colony" where there is tremendous support for one another. Does our organization, department, or team demonstrate this degree of support? Individually, are we as leaders communicating an expectation that this type of support will be provided for each other? And collectively, as a group of leaders, are we building a honey comb of interconnectedness?

2. A beehive culture is based on cooperation and teamwork. The opposite of that is an organization or department where work is isolated into "silos." Is a "silo mentality" preventing the sharing of responsibilities across departments in our organization? As leaders, how might we address this silo mentality and the disconnect between departments or teams?

3. Zync is reminded that there are many tasks in the hive that she does not do. As leaders, how do we communicate this same insight to our employees so they feel needed, engaged and responsible for their contribution? Do we frequently ask them for their expert opinion based on the fact that they do the actual work every day?

4. Is there as much commitment to the whole organization as there is to individual departments, teams or groups? How are we utilizing our *Footprint* and *Unity P-Factors* to build the colony culture?

The Front Porch Philosophy is a way of looking at responsibility and accountability as a behavior that every employee accepts as they cross the 'porch' to their organization.

4. The Front Porch Philosophy

Give Away Control of the Job

Strategy began, "Have you noticed, Zync, that each bee is given great control over the jobs it has? If they walk by a full honey cell, they cap it. If an empty cell needs cleaning, they clean it. This 'self-control,' being able to decide what is needed on their own, increases the amount of self-discipline they bring to the job. They proudly own their work and appreciate it more when you ask them about it rather than when you tell them what you think. This level of engagement with you, as the leader, increases the accountability of every worker in the hive."

"But how do they know what to do?" Zync questioned. "Won't I need to tell them each and every day what their tasks and assignments will be?"

"Oh, no," Belief said, "they have learned to look around their environment and see what needs to be done and what is missing. Identifying what is missing acts as a cue or *prompt* for the bees to know that there is work still to be completed. As soon as they notice the *prompt*, they know exactly how to respond. They have been given the *right of accountability* to do what needs to be done without having to ask for permission. Then as you move throughout the hive, your *Footprint P-Factor* will communicate recognition and reward for a job well done. Your leadership presence helps remind us of the social

35

agreement we have with you as our leader and with each other and how it is all interconnected through trust."

Suddenly Strategy interrupted. "It's time for me to go, my friends. The queen has taken flight! I have to help her locate a new hive. Zync, best of luck with the rest of your training. I'm confident you'll make a great queen." And with that, Strategy flew off.

Quickly, Zync feels the walls of her cell being torn apart by bees on the outside, and she emerges into the hive. Immediately they attend to her as the new queen, providing her with food and cleaning off the residue from the cell she left behind. Zync is struck by how dark it is inside the hive and realizes that much of what the bees achieve must be done through their sense of touch, smell and sound, as it is very difficult to see.

After the feeding and cleaning are complete, Vision and Belief notice a new maturity in Zync as she begins to gather the drones together for her inaugural flight. The hive is excited about the new queen yet anxious about her leaving the hive so soon with the drones. Zync senses the anxiety of the hive and quickly quiets their fears with her *Calming P-Factor*. Vision and Belief watch from a distance and smile in acknowledgement that Zync has learned her first lessons well.

◄ ►

Shortly after her flight is completed, Queen Zync returns to her hive and lands on the "front porch," where she is greeted by her old friends Vision and Belief.

"Welcome back, Queen Zync. You are now our queen and yet there are still lessons that need to be learned. We were discussing accountability and responsibility in our bee culture—what we call *the Front Porch Philosophy*—before the former queen took flight. We need to get back to your lessons," Vision said.

Your leadership presence helps remind us of the social agreement we have with you as our leader and with each other and how it is all interconnected through trust.

The Front Porch Philosophy

"I can give an example of the *Front Porch Philosophy*," Forager interrupted excitedly, landing beside them on the front porch of the hive. "When I come back to the hive from the field, my sacs are full of nectar and pollen. I land on the front porch and am met by house bees who immediately take the pollen and nectar from me into the cells of the hive. I'm dependent on them taking accountability and removing what I've brought as fast as possible, so that I can go back out while the sun is still up."

"Thanks, Forager, good to hear the *Front Porch Philosophy* from your perspective," Belief said. "Each of us has our own personal *front porch* where we decide what to bring in, take responsibility for, hold ourselves accountable for, and, consciously decide to leave for someone else to do, knowing we cannot be the master of all the work."

"I'm sorry," Zync interrupted, "I'm not sure I understand this *Front Porch Philosophy* very well. Why is it called that?"

"For most everyone, when something lands on the *front porch*— say, a package, work to be done, a to-do list, an email, or even a visitor—they have to decide what to do with it—to bring it in, own it, and deal with it, or not. In our beehive philosophy, we have all agreed to take initiative, bring it in, and accept the responsibility and *right of accountability* for whatever lands on our *front porch*. If we see it, we do it, simple as that. We don't say, 'Well, nobody told me to do it' or 'this is so-and-so's job' or even 'I did it yesterday, so now it's someone else's turn.' Because we all believe in the *Front Porch Philosophy*, we all trust the responsibility and accountability of each other," Belief finished.

The Front Porch + Prompt/ Response/Reward = Accountability

"This is an important concept for the beehive, Zync," Vision continued. "When we receive a *prompt* in our environment, we have a *response* or behavior that we know to follow. The *prompt* might be Forager dropping off the newest pollen or nectar, or the *prompt* might be you hatching out of your cell. These *prompts* are met by standard *responses* we do every time like taking in the pollen and making honey, or in your case when you hatched, cleaning, and feeding you. All the bees understand that by following these *responses* we accomplish more than if we individually decide to do what we want to do or ignore the *prompt*. So, when we see each other taking care of business, whether it's the capped honey or the new bees emerging from their cells, we know that we will survive for another season. We can see our *reward* for the work we do and this keeps us responding to the *prompt in a responsible way.* That's accountability!"

"As I mentioned earlier, it's the idea that we all have made a collective social agreement—or choice—to be self-disciplined and self-directed in our work," Belief added excitedly. "No bee is supervised by another bee because there is no need for that. We all have jobs to do and we do them until a new job is required, and then we shift to that new requirement."

"Our collective success creates a passion and yearning to get the task right and repeat our behavior over and over. Even during tough times—deep in the coldness of winter—we believe in our *Front Porch Philosophy*, even though the actual front porch to the hive is closed. That's because our personal *front porch* is still active, focused on the task at hand—in our case keeping the queen and each other warm and fed," Vision concluded.

"But how do you build that passion and yearning for excellence in the bees?" Zync questioned.

The CAMP Method of Motivation

"That passion and yearning come when we feel competent in our jobs, Zync. That's why we keep the new bees in the house for a time, so they build their *competency* and knowledge about the philosophy, *colony culture*, and workflow of the hive. When they feel competent

39

in their jobs and the beehive culture, they feel committed to the hive's success," Vision said.

"It's more than just competency," Belief added. "For passion and yearning to grow, we must know that what we are individually doing has tremendous *meaning* for the colony. We all need to understand that we are part of something great and unique and that our part matters."

"I'd like to jump in here, if I could," Zync's New Strategy mentor said as she landed next to the group. "I've been listening to Vision and Belief, and I think we need to include something else. We bees get passionate when we see each cell being capped with honey. We can see that we're making *progress*. Even when some of our honey is taken from us and we're left with empty frames again, we know that we can quickly make *progress* if we work together."

"I think giving each bee *autonomy* to decide where and how to move and shift jobs based on what's needed must be important, as well," Zync added. "Bees need to be able to make their own choices to feel important and valued."

"Wow, Zync, I think you're really on to something! Developing in each bee *competency* as well as *autonomy* and ensuring they see *meaningfulness* and *progress* in their work could really motivate the bees in a special way," New Strategy said. "Why don't we call this our CAMP Method for bee motivation? *Competency, Autonomy, Meaningfulness, and Progress* are all fundamental to a bee's motivation and a great way we can retain their spirit, talent, and engagement in our hive!" finished New Strategy.

Vision added, "You're really getting the hang of this, Zync!"

"Yes," Belief said. "Put *CAMP* together with our *Front Porch Philosophy* and *The Prompt-Response-Reward Approach* and we have a great strategy for accountability and engagement!"

"However, Zync," Belief warned, "just because you say it here and now doesn't mean that it is automatically embraced throughout the hive. You must remind us every day with your *Footprint P-Factor* to use our *Front Porch Philosophy,* this new *CAMP Method* and the *PRR Approach,* and we need to see it in you, too. A true leader understands

The Camp Method of Motivation

C - Competency
A - Autonomy
M - Meaningfulness
P - Progress

the necessity of putting promises to actions. These actions over time form habits. Habits done long enough become the character of the hive and the character of the hive, Zync, will be your legacy. Just because we talk here and now doesn't mean that you've implemented anything yet. Not to discourage you, but to encourage you—follow through with your promises until they become actions, let your actions form habits, and let the character of the hive you build be your lasting legacy."

"Thanks, Belief, that's something to really think about."

The Front Porch Philosophy Reflections for Today's Leaders

There is much to learn from the beehive in this chapter. The bees move together from one job to another completing tasks without specific direction.

The Prompt-Response-Reward Approach

This *"Prompt-Response-Reward"* approach can be designed in organizations as the leader identifies the *'prompts'*—such as an upset customer, a late order, a decrease in orders or revenue, a nonconformance, or simply work to be done—which trigger *responses* to occur for everyone within the organization. A skilled leader defines the key *prompts* for the organization and then teaches what *responses*—or standard work—must follow. Further, the leader ensures that *rewards* or recognition occur, causing the desire to repeat the behavior to build. Celebrating and rewarding successes is important too!

At times we may find it necessary as leaders to prioritize our *responses* in relationship to the *prompt* based on the resources that we have. For example, we may have a long list of projects that have to be completed for our division or department and everything looks like it's a top priority. As the leader, our job is to prioritize those tasks to the vital few that will achieve what is needed—especially when there is great pressure from outside the group.

There is tremendous traffic on the front porch of a beehive, almost like what you would see on our busiest airport runways. The accountability to show up on time, ready to go, is something all leaders can demonstrate themselves and expect in others. Most importantly, we mustn't give up our *Front Porch Philosophy* and take back the responsibility and accountability when the pressure builds. Rather, we should shift the philosophy into high gear by helping our workers define the short term focus, narrowing the *prompts* to just a critical few. We can define the required *response* and clearly identify the *rewards* that will occur. For example, if the budget department *prompts* us with a low receivables' notice for this month, what should the short-term *response* be on our part and the organization's part? It might be staying later hours; it might be galvanizing the workforce to go out and get more sales. For many organizations the *reward* in this case may simply be to survive.

The CAMP Method of Motivation

The bees stay stimulated in their own work because the jobs are designed instinctually to provide the *CAMP* method of motivation—*Competency, Autonomy, Meaningfulness* and *Progress*. This same pattern can be implemented by leadership in every job within every organization. When employees arrive and leave each day, they pass the symbolic *front porch* of the organization and know, from this prompt, the level of accountability and responsibility they have been given and must assume. It is also a promise by leadership to help the workers seek out competency, autonomy, progress, and meaningfulness. Part of the dedication to the *Front Porch Philosophy* is that the *CAMP Method* is ensured for every employee. Trusting in the commitment of the organization to a *Front Porch Philosophy* and *CAMP Method* is paramount to your success as a leader. A leader who spends time on employee development—or coaching discussions—can use the *CAMP Method* to see what is present or missing for each employee's motivational needs.

The accountability to show up, on time, ready to go is something all leaders can demonstrate themselves and expect in others.

Delegating Responsibility

When Forager is met at the front porch of the hive by bees ready and willing to carry the heavy load, Forager trusts that others are working as hard to make the hive successful. This delegation of responsibility is critical to your success as a leader and is often where leaders fall short. Trying to do it all, or thinking that no one can do it as well as you, can be a leader's downfall. The beehive recognizes that shared values, shared responsibility, shared accountability and the *CAMP Method* of motivation are instrumental to the hive's survival.

Consistency in Approach

Before they part Belief presses Zync, mentioning that leadership is not about long speeches or promises not kept, but the action and consistent commitment behind those promises that creates a leader's lasting legacy. This striking commitment to habitually do the same things over and over is remarkable in the hive. Leaders today would benefit from finding their best "groove," then consistently delivering it, day after day. It is often the consistency and discipline that are lacking, especially as leaders are tossed around by the winds of change.

Group Discussion Questions

1. Have we established a *Front Porch Philosophy* in our organization so that every day when employees go in and out of the organization, department, or team they are reminded and reinforced in their responsibility and *right of accountability*?
2. Is there a "shared load" value system in place? Do we make it clear that mediocre or uncommitted behavior is not acceptable?
3. How are we encouraging new employees to take their role

in the "hive" and suggesting to "experienced" employees to mentor and train others?

4. How have we built a *CAMP Method* (Competency, Autonomy, Meaningfulness, and Progress) into every job in our organization so that direct supervision is not required, and employee motivation and retention are sought after?

5. Are we encouraging delegated accountability, as a *predictable behavior* pattern? Have we identified the *prompt-response-reward method* (PRR) to standardize the way work should be accomplished? Do we have a reward system that is meaningful to our employees?

6. Are we tolerating and even spending our limited time and energy on employees who have not committed to our *survival of the hive* culture and philosophy, or who let down others in the accomplishment of their tasks? If so, how will we address this inequity?

5. Bee-2-Bee Waggle Dance

"Zync, it's time to talk about the importance of communication within the beehive," Strategy suggested. "I'd like to introduce you to Scout, one of our dancing bees."

"We dance?" Zync asked incredulously. "Yes," Scout explained, "my job is to leave the hive first and scout the region for the best sources of pollen and nectar. I may fly many miles until I locate the best source. When I return to the hive, I dance to let the other foraging bees know where the nectar and pollen are located."

"Can you show me how you do this dance?"

"Sure. First, I walk straight ahead, vigorously shaking my abdomen and producing a buzzing sound with the beat of my wings. Pay close attention to how far and how fast I walk, because that indicates how far off the nectar is. Then I align my body in the direction of the food, relative to the sun, making a figure-eight movement," Scout explained, demonstrating the movement to Zync.

"That's a lot of movement, Scout," said Zync.

"That's why we call it the *Bee-2-Bee Waggle Dance*," Scout replied. "As I repeat this pattern over and over at the end of each scouting mission, the foraging bees know exactly how to find the flower source of our food. When we waggle our bodies, the scent of the flower spreads through the hive and the smell communicates to the foragers exactly what flower to harvest. Quite amazing, isn't it?"

Communication is not some special event or missive that goes out once a month to the hive. We initiate communication throughout the hive every minute of every day with our Bee-2-Bee Waggle Dance.

"I'm impressed with how quickly you communicate the possibilities and opportunities out there with others in the hive. It gives us accurate information so we don't waste time looking for things you already know. I see that not only do I communicate through the *P-Factors*, but you communicate through your waggle dance."

Scout added, "We also communicate about the flower with the other bees in the field by leaving behind a positive charge on the flower which tells the other bees that the pollen is gone."

"You see, Zync," Belief said, "communication is not some special event or missive that goes out once a month to the hive. We initiate communication throughout the hive and in the field every minute of every day. We are all dependent on each other to communicate bee-to-bee, both from you and to you. If Scout comes back and there is no dance, it is our job to communicate to you that flower production has ceased outside the hive. Then you will need to communicate to us when we must cluster together for the winter months to stay warm."

"I'm surprised that Scout would feel comfortable bringing discouraging news back to the hive. Isn't Scout afraid that the hive, or I as queen, would be angry?"

Critical News Is Not Bad News

"Never, Zync," Belief explained, "That would assume that critical news is bad news and should be hidden. We don't operate that way. We bring all news to the hive as critical for our survival and then we work together to determine how to respond to it. We're not afraid of communicating."

"We don't question whether the bearer of the news is right or wrong, because the bee would not communicate the news unless the bee was correct. We don't allow rumors and gossip in the hive, as they are detrimental to our communication system and our *colony culture*," Belief added.

"I suppose part of this requires that I listen well to the news within the hive, coming from the front porch through our scouts and foragers. If I act like I'm the only one who should be communicating, then that's a big mistake, isn't it? I need to realize that many bees in our colony have information to share that will support our efforts for survival."

"Exactly, Zync. Communication involves listening and speaking. Both sides have to work hard at it, and we all must trust one another to deliver accurate information. No bee will tell you something that isn't true. And every bee will believe everything you say. There is no second-guessing in a beehive."

Communicating in Real Time

Vision continued, "We communicate in real time, not waiting for an emergency or trouble to encourage our communication but communicating at all times. This is the true power and strength of our hive. Every minute we are communicating in some fashion."

"As you know by the *Waggle Dance*," Scout added, "we send each other continuous, non-verbal cues all day long. Whether it's me communicating about a found source of food, or it's Forager communicating to the worker bee to empty the saddle bags, or the sister bee calling for a grooming session or it's you providing your *Footprint, Calming and Unity P-Factors,* each and every bee takes responsibility for communication. The responsibility for communication is not yours alone, Zync. We all need the communication cues from one another to make the organization of the hive a success."

Zync's eyes lit up. "I see! We're an interconnected community that cues each other all day long through our various communication systems. It is only the strength of our network, the discipline to listen to one another, and the continuous encouragement of feedback that keeps this hive alive!"

"Furthermore," Belief said, "we communicate nonverbally through our smell, sound, sight, and taste. The sight of the *Waggle Dance,* the speed of our wings flapping, and the taste of certain pollens are extremely important to us. We use these communication channels—movement, odor cues, and food exchanges—to share information. All these intricate communications help us to determine the next steps we need to take to ensure our survival."

The B-2-B Waggle Dance Reflections for Today's Leaders

Aristotle was one of the first to study the complex yet elegant communication systems, or dance, of the honeybee. Many activities in the beehive focus on communication, which is often considered the foundation of their socialization. Just open the top of a hive and you can imagine the vast amount of communication that is occurring to move this huge organization through its seasons. The smell and taste of honey, the buzzing, the wings flapping—all signals of health and wellbeing to the hive. Interestingly, the pitch of the buzzing changes when the bees sense danger.

Since bees don't have the emotional complexity of humans, they are able to simply and honestly report on exact conditions. As humans we need to strive toward the same clear, direct communication without regard for the nature of the news, our own expectations and assumptions, or any other number of factors that make communication for us so difficult. If we could approach communication with the simplicity of a bee's approach, we might be better off.

The BUZZ

Too often, as leaders we tend to limit our communication to an "as needed" basis, or in response to crises emerging, only to find out that our communication system is not the well-oiled machine we need it to be. The beehive teaches us that instead, we should focus on creating a sociality—or intercommunity *BUZZ* of an ongoing, organic communication where discussion, thought, and feedback are all second nature within our groups, teams, and organizations. Some organizations today are endorsing this philosophy through social media networks that create and manage ongoing organizational conversations.

The bee's *Waggle Dance* sends critical information to the hive similar to how a manager or supervisor might take his/her leader's communication and spread it throughout the department. What's going on out there? Where are the best resources for us? How can I help you find exactly what you need? Here's why what you're doing is so important to us.

We must set up a communication expectation where information is freely shared throughout our "hive"—top-down, bottom-up, and crisscross—in order to ensure maximum knowledge and accurate information transfer are present. As organizations we must practice and refine the very communication systems that help facilitate information to the whole organization on a daily basis.

In many cases we have placed the emphasis on getting tasks done or delivering a project, with inadequate attention paid to building the communication plan to get there. How do we communicate under normal conditions? And what do we communicate when the situation is extreme? Too often our communication is "a day late, and a dollar short," convincing employees that the grapevine is a better source than leadership. In that way—utilizing our grapevine—we are very similar to the bees.

Let's face it—we all have our own distinct *waggle dance*, a series of verbal and non-verbal messages that we send out every day. Some of us "waggle" a very confusing, disconnected, "I-focused" message that disengages others. Our body language may be closed and distant, or domineering and dictatorial. It's still a *waggle dance*. On the other hand, some leaders waggle a message that is so vibrant, clear, and engaging that we immediately want to follow and support them. As leaders we should definitely know the quality of our *waggle dance* and its impact on others.

The BUZZ is an ongoing, organic communication
where discussion, thought, and feedback are
all second nature within our groups, teams
and organizations.

Group Discussion Questions

1. What is our organization's internal *Waggle Dance* that alerts everyone to opportunities and possibilities that would benefit their work? What does the *BUZZ* in our organization sound like? Negative, positive, or silent? What systems have we set up that create an ongoing, organic form of communication?

2. How are we as leaders encouraging all information, good or bad, to be shared with us and among our employees? How are we overcoming the blocks or bottlenecks in our communication flow?

3. Are we listening to the "buzzing of our bees" as much as we're talking to them? Is there a surplus of trust in our organization, department, or team so much so that no worker will tell us something that isn't true or correct? If not, why not, and how would we start to address this trust deficit?

4. How will we relinquish the full responsibility of communication and allow the whole of our hive to share the effort with us in order to make communication a real-time event? Have we established an ongoing network of real-time communication?

5. As a leader, am I known for my communication ability? Do I work hard at delivering clear and thoughtful messages with my spoken word and my body language in alignment? Does my written communication promote sociality as well? Knowing that every leader has a waggle dance, what does mine look like?

6. The Perfect Product

"Of course, Zync, the reason we work so hard, communicate so well and listen to each other intently is to produce the perfect product, our honey. It is this end goal, communicated to all, that drives the disciplined action of the hive," instructed Vision.

"At this point, I'd like to introduce one of our newest bees, House Bee, who will take us to the production floor of our hive to show you the reward for all this hard work," said New Strategy.

"Hi ya, Queen Zync! Proud to have you with us. I'm one of many house bees charged with securing and producing a perfect product flow. I'll be showing you around our production and storage facilities," greeted House Bee.

As Zync and the group entered the main chamber, or super of the hive, the overwhelming smell and fragrance of the honey was inescapable.

"Wow, this truly is amazing. Look at all the honey here!" gasped Zync, as she surveyed the clear, golden liquid oozing from the uncapped, open cells.

House Bee added, "Our high-quality honey can be distinguished by fragrance, taste, and consistency. The work doesn't stop as the foragers come in with pollen or even as we churn the pollen into honey. Our honey is not complete until we make the perfect product. We work hard to make sure as much water, or defect, is out of the honey as physically possible."

The Perfect Product

"Let's start from the beginning of the process so you can see and understand the whole production flow of our perfect product," House Bee suggested.

"At the beginning of the process flow, our bees obtain nectar by sucking it out of flowers and storing it in their special honey stomach which we call our "nectar backpack." After visiting between 150 to 1500 flowers, the honey stomach is full and almost equal in weight to the bee itself. At this point the forager bee laboriously returns to the hive with its load."

"Heads up! Comin' through!" said a large and rather colorful forager bee as it flew past the group lumbering under its heavy load.

"That bee was in such a rush! Why was it flying so oddly?" asked Zync.

"Some of our forager bees return to the hive not with nectar but with pollen. Our forager bees have hair-like "baskets" on their hind legs, and it is into these that they pack pollen grains while visiting flowers. As you can see by that bee over there, you can easily identify pollen-carrying bees from our nectar-carrying ones because of the brightly-colored orange and yellow pollen packed into their baskets," House Bee said.

"They fly like that because of the oversized loads of pollen that they carry. We refer to this raw material as 'bee-bread' and use it to feed our next cycle of brood," Vision added.

"Fascinating, the complexity of the hive and what goes into our perfect product," Zync said.

"Oh, it doesn't stop there. As Forager drops off the nectar, which is nearly 80 percent water, our worker bees process it working long hours," Vision explained.

"Do they ever complain?" asked Zync.

"No, because of your leadership they know their purpose and the importance of what they do. Their purpose is to create the perfect product, so the hive can survive in the winter. We work with the end goal in mind, making sure we have enough honey stored," chimed in Belief.

"As I was saying," House Bee continued, "once we've processed the nectar, we deposit it on the upper side of a cell wall and await its final conversion into honey. This conversion is largely an evaporation process which we quicken by moving air across the honey comb, fanning our wings in a coordinated effort."

"What's our moisture count today?" Vision asked House Bee.

"I'd say we're at about 17 percent today, Vision," reported House Bee.

"Seventeen percent! Down from 80 percent originally!" exclaimed Zync.

"What was our moisture count yesterday?" Vision asked.

"We were at 17 percent," House Bee confirmed.

"And the day before that?"

"Also 17 percent."

"And the week before that?"

"Again, 17 percent."

Vision looked at Zync smiling and gave a wink.

"Zync, we call it the perfect product not because we get it down to 1 percent, but because we work every day in pursuit of excellence by holding consistently at 17 percent. A moisture count of 1 percent would not work, nor would 25 percent. We know that the perfect product requires 17 percent moisture count. So day in and day out, we make sure our honey has that much—no more, no less. This is our perfect product."

"How do you know every bee is committed to working to get 17 percent? How do you know everyone wants to work to get a perfect product? How can one bee trust that another bee is going to show up or do its end of the work?" asked Zync.

Perfect Product Honey Stream

Belief laughed. "Those are a lot of questions, Zync! But I think I might have the answer. You see we're all part of the *Perfect Product Honey Stream*. It's important for every bee to see the big picture. They need to see how they fit into the whole stream of honey production. From Scout, who finds the supply, to Forager, who gets the raw material and brings it to the hive, to those of us, including House Bee, within the hive who unload it on the porch, transfer it inside, convert it into honey, seal it, and package it for the future. That is our *Perfect Product Honey Stream*. It's important that we see the flow of the whole process, like a stream from beginning to end. Each bee is committed to one another, because we understand that this is the only way the *Perfect Product Honey Stream* works. We must communicate effectively with one another, share the burden when necessary, and eventually sacrifice everything if required to do so."

"Sacrifice everything?" Zync questioned hesitantly.

"We'll get to that part later, Zync," Vision said.

"We are very careful the way we treat all components of the *Perfect Product Honey Stream*. Even flower, which has no other role than supplying the raw material, is treated with the utmost care and respect. We do not go out and destroy the source of our honey but gently extract it with precision without damage to the flower," House Bee said.

The Internal Customer

"Equally, as we all have different roles and responsibilities in the *Perfect Product Honey Stream*, we see each other as internal customers dependent on each other's work. Let me show you our *Perfect Product Honey Stream* map over here which illustrates how everything fits together. We show each new bee our *Perfect Product Honey Stream* map so they learn how the whole process works and how important each bee's effort is to the whole stream. We also use our map to discuss where we're having problems in our honey flow, especially when it gets very busy and we're trying to complete the cells and frames quickly before winter," Belief noted.

It's important for every bee to see the big picture. They need to see how they fit into the whole stream of honey production.

The Rhythm to the Perfect Product Honey Stream

"Within our organization, there is a certain rhythm we want to achieve when making the perfect product. If 1,000 foragers land on the front porch at one time and only 100 worker bees are there to meet them, our *Perfect Product Honey Stream* would be backed up and not work. Then we'd need to store the nectar and pollen outside the hive, which we aren't able to do. And the House Bees would feel frantic trying to keep up when it would be impossible to do so. It's important for us to achieve the correct rhythm that is most effective for everyone along the *Perfect Product Honey Stream*," Vision illustrated, pointing to each work process on the map.

"When the clover blooms in the spring, or the goldenrod flowers in early autumn, our production flow has to magnify tremendously and still be perfect to meet the heightened demand for processing. That's why we use our *Perfect Product Honey Stream System* to guide our quality, speed, process, and outputs," House Bee said.

"You as queen need to understand the *Perfect Product Honey Stream System*," Belief stressed. "When you communicate to the other bees, they need to know that you know how the process works. If they think you are too far removed from the *Perfect Product Honey Stream* process to know what they're suggesting or are worried about, they will doubt and resent your leadership."

"I'm just curious about why you all keep emphasizing the Perfect Product. Isn't it okay to just have uncapped honey in each cell? It seems like added work to take all the water out and then cap each cell. We're just going to eat it in a few months anyway."

"Who do you think our customers are, Zync?" Belief asked.

"Hmmm. If a customer is anyone who depends on our work, I suppose our customers are all of us, right?" Zync replied.

"Well, would you be happy in the dead of winter with watered-down honey, as the customer?" Belief questioned.

"I wouldn't want watered-down honey ever, let alone in the dead of winter!" Zync blurted out.

"Exactly," Belief said. "You expect the perfect honey product every time, and why shouldn't you? This is the hard work of your leadership. The same is true for every other bee. They expect a perfect honey product at the end of each day and into the winter months. There is a performance expectation among every bee to work to create that perfect honey product, regardless of the job we're doing. Each job is an important link to our perfect product. If we know that our honey requires 17 percent water count, why would we accept anything different?

As our leader you need to reinforce our commitment to the perfection of our honey even when we're rushing to make a lot of it and when we have all the mono- and multi-floral lines in production. We still need to know your commitment to both quality and speed. Quality cannot be compromised for speed, and yet keeping the *Perfect Product Honey Stream* moving is paramount. It is a very delicate balance, and yet one that determines whether our hive will survive."

◄ ►

Just then, there was a terrifyingly loud crack that sounded like the hive was being split in two.

Suddenly, the top of the hive was opened and a large figure in white peered in. With its large hands, it pried off the top frame of the hive.

Rriippp!

Sunlight streamed into the hive.

"What's going on?" asked Zync anxiously.

"The figure in white is taking some of our honey. It's okay. This is part of the process as we have come to know it. This is the beekeeper, who helps us in the spring before the flowers have blossomed by providing sugar water for us; in return, we give the beekeeper some of our honey. The beekeeper never takes all the honey, because then we would not survive through the winter. The beekeeper returns the frames empty, and we will begin again," Vision yelled over the thundering movement of the whole hive.

"Oh no …" Belief said in horror. "This is more than just a visit from the beekeeper!"

That instant, a band of robber bees flying at breakneck speed and aiming right for the front porch emerged from behind the beekeeper.

"Battle stations, everyone!" yelled the guard bees, sending out the *Alarm P-Factor.*

The Perfect Production Honey Stream
Reflections for Today's Leaders

A beehive is very much like the production floor of a manufacturing site or a very busy office complex. People are going back and forth, moving product or service along the various stages of the process flow. Bees know how to make the perfect product, working together to add enzymes to the nectar and then extracting the water by fanning their wings. When the honey is perfect it is capped with wax. If a bee moves over an uncapped cell, the bee will check its perfection and then cap it. There is no such thing as producing an imperfect product for a honey bee. It would be contrary to every instinct in their body. The notion of a lesser quality product being "good enough" does not exist in a beehive.

Many employees are not always clear about what a Perfect Product is in their world. If an email has spelling errors, does that really matter? If financial calculations don't add up, what's the big deal? If a process is completed out of conformance to the standard, who really cares? We count up the errors and then see rework as normal to correct a problem. Many times, we focus on symptoms rather than roots of the problems, repeating the errors over and over as failure costs mount. Other times, what is considered less than perfect one day inexplicably becomes acceptable when the rush is on. This mixed message confuses employees about the true Perfect Product standard that must be achieved. Leadership must be clear that the Perfect Product standard does not vary based on production volume or speed. Likewise, quality should never be compromised to achieve speed. Leadership must examine the ground floor messages about quality and speed that employees share among each other.

Leadership has a tendency to distance from the process heartbeat of the organization or department. They grow out of touch with the day-to-day operations and are so focused on their own work that they don't see the connection to the workplace culture they are responsible for creating.

Yet, if leadership stood back and watched their own *Perfect Product System*, many insights might emerge. It might be clear that no one really talks to each other as the work is being performed. It might be apparent that a new worker is not well trained and competent. The experienced worker may have detached from process flow out of disinterest, boredom, or feeling devalued over time. The leader must observe all these nuances in the environment and put them together into a *Perfect Product Honey Stream System* that corrects the roots of the problem.

Likewise, many employees in organizations are not fully aware of each step in the flow of product or service through the organization. As a result, they fail to see and know the big picture—or what we call here the *Perfect Product Honey Stream System*. They only know their small part. Also, they don't always see that they have customers before, after and even among themselves. As leaders we must speak to the importance of customers, even when they are difficult, demanding, or dislike us. As Zync states, "Anyone who depends on our work is our customer." When all this is put together, whether in a team, department, or an entire organization, the recognition of interdependence is inescapable.

The leadership role is to understand fully the entire process, even when it involves thousands of little processes and then to be able to build those linkages and synapses between each process in the *Perfect Product System*. This cannot be done from a geographical or emotional distance. There is much for a leader to learn by working on an assembly line, handling work orders in maintenance, or manning the customer service phone in a call center. If you don't know the job, you can't manage the job and lead others.

Leadership must be clear that the Perfect Product standard does not vary based on production volume or speed. Likewise, quality should never be compromised to achieve speed.

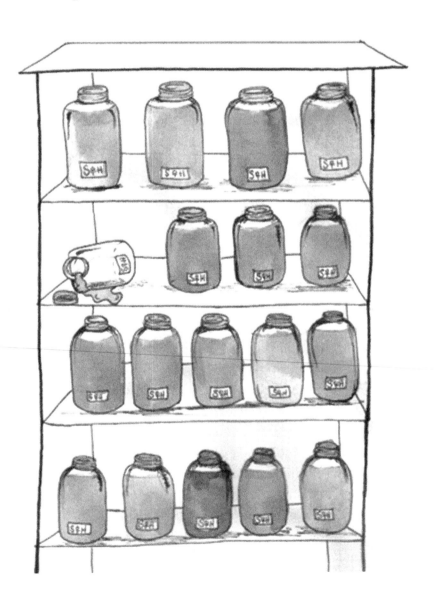

Most importantly, the mentality of creating a perfect product begins with the leader and how that leader performs. If a leader is not demonstrating his or her own "perfect leadership product," then how can they expect others to be committed to a perfect product approach themselves? We have seen leaders excuse their own behavior— outbursts, inattention to detail, micromanaging, and even working on the wrong things—as acceptable and then turn and point out the mistakes of others. We have seen leaders who develop huge metric systems to track all the problems in the product or service flow and yet never go and ask the worker for his or her input. Even better, would the leader take on the job for half a day to fully understand why the system is broken?

Old models of distant, command and control leadership will not work in a world of constant change, increasing demands and a multi-generational, multi-cultural workforce. Everyone must be a valuable part of the solution to the *survival of the hive.*

Group Discussion Questions

1. As leaders, how much of our focus has been on the satisfaction of the customer, remembering, like the bees, that our employees are our customers as well? Do we teach employees that they have customers within their own workplace that depend on their work, and those customers have an standard they expect to receive?

2. Do our employees have a clear understanding of what the Perfect Product or Perfect Service is in their own work flow? Is our message ever confusing to them, or do we shift messages based on the crisis of the moment? Is waste and rework tolerated and excused?

3. Are we, as leaders, familiar with the *Perfect Product Honey Stream System* in our organization, beyond just our own department or team? Have we mapped it out for all to see?

Do we observe the processes we oversee to identify what are missing or broken?

4. When did we last do some of the jobs in our workplace to increase our understanding of the requirements and frustrations of the job, or what in the system might be broken?

5. Is building a product or service that is "good enough" acceptable, or are we in constant pursuit of the "perfect product or service" within our industry?

6. Do we benchmark against the best and avoid an insular, "not invented here" attitude?

7. Protect the Hive

As the robber bees launched their attack and the *Attack* and *Repel P-Factor Alarms* blared, the defender bees surrounded Zync. She shouted frantically to Vision and New Strategy, "What do I need to do? Should I fly out with them? Tell me what to do!"

With bees flying everywhere to their battle stations and the pitch of the *BUZZ* changing dramatically, Vision commanded, "Zync, you are not to go out there! We need to get you to the command center for protection. Our bees are all aware that we cannot risk losing your leadership. This is the last and final lesson for you. The bees will do their very best to protect and defend the ideals of the hive that your leadership has built. Each bee commits to sacrifice what it needs to for the *survival of the hive*, just as the former queen sacrificed half her hive when she left to ensure our future. Your function is to assess the initial loss, decide how to allocate new resources and build up our hive again by using all of your P-Factors."

As New Strategy, Vision, and Belief took her to the command center, the defending bees sounded the rallying cry, "To the *survival of the hive!*"

◄ ►

Survival of the hive is a shared responsibility, a culture built on accountability for the sake of the whole, and a code of dependability among every bee, including the queen.

At the command center Zync witnessed the actions of the attack. She saw not only the guard bees, but also House Bee, Forager, Scout and, others all coming together to attack the intruders. All the bees were leaving their normal posts to help defend the hive. To her amazement, she saw the precise coordination of the bees as they attacked the intruding robber bees.

Leaving the Post

"How do they all know to rally to the action when the hive is under attack?" asked Zync.

"We call this *Leaving the Post*. Every bee knows to help every other bee when we are under attack," instructed Defender Bee.

Defender continued, "It would not be right for us to continue to do our own work while other bees are threatened or overwhelmed. We also understand that any crack in the colony or breach of our defenses provides an opening for the robbing to begin."

"What's our plan of survival?" Zync asked somewhat aggressively.

"You'll see that some of the bees form a guard around the honey in order to protect it. You'll sense them using their *Repel P-Factor*. Likewise, we have a counter-insurgence team that, alerted by the *Attack P-Factor*, move in against the intruders. We have a dual-defense system, one being focused on defending the hive and one being focused on attacking intruders. We leave nothing to chance!" New Strategy explained.

The 4R Approach: Report, Research, Respond, Recover

"How did they all know we were under attack? Before I even knew what was going on, our defense system was in high alert," Zync asked.

"We apply a *4R Approach*, Zync, when in either Repel or Attack mode: *Report, Research, Respond*, and *Recover*. We investigate the situation, report our findings, and decide how to respond. When the attack is over, we will do our analysis of what worked or didn't as we recover."

"Let me illustrate," Defender Bee began, "usually a couple of robber bees are spotted on the front porch of the hive by our guard bees. The guard bees sense danger and release the *Alarm P-Factors*—that's the *Report* part. Can you smell the banana-like odor? That's our *Alarm P-Factor*. This odor alerted all the other bees to stop work and investigate the cause of the alarm—the *Research* part. Our first response is crucial because if the robber bees sense a weak hive, they will tell other bees to come and then mayhem will follow. Our *Repel P-Factor* warns the guard bees to escort the robbers out of the hive if there are just a few—our *Response*. If that doesn't work, the *Attack P-Factor* authorizes the guard bees to kill the intruders. Afterwards, we will debrief on what happened and make changes if needed—the *Recover* part. We practice this behavior over and over during our *Front Porch Philosophy* and *Prompt-Response-Reward* training."

"Zync, what's wrong? You look concerned," Defender Bee noted.

"Well, I'm just wondering—won't the bees be upset if I am in the command center and not helping them to defend the hive?" puzzled Zync.

"Zync, we do not operate in an 'us versus them' mentality. We do not see you as a 'them'—separate from us—and I don't believe you see us that way either. I know you have been taught by the others about the *Unity P-Factor* and how closely we all work together for the good of the hive. You are in the command center because you carry the future of the hive within you. Protection of this future will be your contribution to this fight. If we were to allow you to die in the fight, the entire hive would be destroyed. We know how important your leadership is to us and to the future, so much so that we, without hesitation, will sacrifice ourselves to defend it. There may come a time, when the fight is nearing the end that we need you to show your *Footprint P-Factor*, your *Calming P-factor* and *Unity*

The 4R Approach:

Report, Research, Respond, and Recover

P-Factor leadership to help us restore the hive to normalcy. And your *Resourcing P-Factor* will help us rebuild, as we are certain to lose many bees," Defender Bee encouraged Zync.

As this truth dawned on Zync, she said, "This is what Belief was talking about when she mentioned 'a sacrifice when the time comes.' We all must sacrifice at times for the good of the hive. Sometimes it will be to protect leadership or other members of the hive, other times the sacrifice will be in rebuilding the hive for the future—but we all have a responsibility to sacrifice what is necessary for the *survival of the hive*."

It became clear to Zync: *survival of the hive* is a shared responsibility, a culture built on accountability for the sake of the whole, and a code of dependability among every bee, including the queen. It is a bond of trust between a queen and her bees.

Protect the Hive Reflections for Today's Leaders

As a leader, you may be wondering, "Why are we talking about attacks? We're never under attack." If we step back and think about it, organizations are under at least two types of attack: internal attacks that occur within the organization as departments, teams or individuals compete with each other and allow an "us vs. them" mentality to form between leadership and the workforce. You notice in the beehive culture that internal attacks between the bees or the bees and the queen never occur. To a bee, it makes no sense to attack another bee that is working hard for the same purpose.

The other type of attack is an external attack, caused by something on the outside that threatens the organization, team or department. There are many types of attacks from the outside: competitors stealing intellectual property, disgruntled customers telling other customers, cyber-attacks, price increases for materials and transportation, unhappy stockholders affecting market share, changing regulations and legislation, even different sites competing with each other for resources.

Some of these attacks require the *Repel Alarm* (focused on protection and minimizing the impact on the organization, department or team). Some require the *Attack Alarm* when everyone must come together to address the attack and support the organization's survival. The *4-R Strategy* works for both types of attacks: *Report, Research, Respond, and Recover.* For example, if a negative comment is made on a social media, the approach would be to Report it first, Research the legitimacy of the claim and how you want to address it, Respond to the decision made, and then Recover, by assessing whether the Response addressed the Report. The *4R Method* works for any repel or attack situation.

We also see in this chapter how the bees protect leadership from the attack. Zync is protected because she carries all the bee eggs for the future of the hive. In organizations leadership needs to be protected because it carries the Strategy, Vision, and Belief that will ensure the future of the organization. There are some well-known organizations that have dismissed their leadership, only to bring them back again when they realize that the strategy, vision, and beliefs have gone off track. Once an organization has the leadership it needs to achieve its height of success, it must be careful to protect that leadership from outside attack, including against robbers, who will try to steal the leadership talent away.

An important understanding in this chapter is the *Leaving Your Post* mentality which encourages employees to fend off an attack, whether in their area of expertise or not, for the sake of the whole. It is very troublesome today to see employees remain in their own silos and not respond to the immediate needs of a troubled department or team because it is not in their area. The notion of "we're all in this together" is a philosophy the bees can teach us all.

Most importantly, bees have a method in place which unites and protects the hive against attackers. They don't wait until the attack is underway to decide how to respond; they have been equipped from the beginning to defend themselves and attack when needed. As leaders we need to determine, in advance, how we will respond to attacks on our people, teams, departments, or organizations whether from within or externally. What defenses will we use? What stingers do we have in place? And then we need to unite in an agreed-to approach to overpower what threatens our survival.

Group Discussion Questions

1. What attacks our organization internally? Do we have an "us vs. them" mentality? Do we have resistors to change that deplete our spirit of teamwork and unity? How do we respond to such situations?

2. How do we respond to the outside attacks? Do we emit an Attack or Repel alarm, making it clear the nature of the attack and the need for response? Are we using our alarms effectively and to the correct degree?

3. When a serious attack occurs do we lead by example and encourage our employees to have a *Leaving the Post* mentality where they get out of their silos to help other employees who are under attack? Do we share resources between departments to address the attack? Do we support and help other leaders who are under attack?

4. Throughout the attack the leader may need to be issuing the *Unity, Calming, Resourcing, and Footprint P-Factors* to keep the organization or department focused and united. Resources will need to be redistributed to align with current needs. How are these characteristics demonstrated in our leadership when the organization, department or team is under attack?

5. How do we use the *4-R Strategy (Research, Report, Respond, and Recover)* as leaders when faced with external or internal attacks? Are we careful to research and report the facts before responding? Do our leaders know how to respond when an attack occurs, or are they guessing?

6. Do we devote time to discuss the lessons learned after the event and what we will need to do to recover our strength for the future?

8. The Season of a Hive

For everything there is a season, and a time for every matter under heaven: a time to be born, and a time to die; a time to plant, and a time to pluck up what is planted; a time to kill, and a time to heal; a time to break down, and a time to build up.

—Ecclesiastes 3:1–3

The beehive analogy illustrates for us a number of key points that relate to leadership. Bees know that there is a season and purpose to everything they do. Spring is a dangerous time for bees as their honey cells are empty and the hive is at its lowest population. No flowers have emerged and the bees struggle to stay alive. Many times forager bees will have to travel substantial distances to find nectar and pollen. Meanwhile, the queen lays upwards of 2,000 eggs per day to populate the hive, as it builds up to summertime total of over 50,000 bees all working together to complete the multitude of tasks required of the hive. This massive amount of energy is set in motion and accomplished through an instinctual communication network of smell, sound, sight and taste.

The queen bee exemplifies several key leadership attributes that organizational leaders today would be wise to emulate. Through the queen's pheromone system—or P-Factors as we have called them here—the queen can unify, calm, assure, and resource the hive. She

For everything there is a season,
and a time for every matter under heaven:
a time to be born,
and a time to die;
a time to plant,
and a time to pluck up what is planted;
a time to kill,
and a time to heal;
a time to break down,
and a time to build up.

is well aware that the job of producing resources for the hive is hers alone. Many times leaders are so removed from where the resources are needed in the department, team or organization, they are not able to recognize and negotiate or claim the resources they need. Instead, they end up being a leader who takes away resources from where they are needed, without a clear understanding of the risks involved.

This book was written out of our commitment to the idea of *survival of the hive* and our concern about leadership today. We, as leaders, have lost focus on the imperative of survival as we become so absorbed in managing the day-to-day plethora of changes each of us faces. Queen Zync personifies the stewardship and servanthood that is needed by leaders to create and sustain the vision, strategy and beliefs within an organization. Many organizations today experience trust bankruptcy because of downsizing, corruption, politics, and leaders' self-serving survival. Employees are suspicious and cynical about leadership; they don't believe in leadership.

Survival of the Hive has focused on the basics of how to recalibrate the leadership in your organization, through seven basic tools of leadership:

Survival of the Hive: An obsession with what is good for the whole organization over what is good for any person, department or team. Vision, strategy, and belief help define "due north" so everyone is committed to the greater purpose, direction, and philosophy.

The P-Factors: Strong leadership attributes that are practiced every day and become characteristic of all leaders in the organization. The leader's *footprint*, the ability to *calm* and *unify*, the strength to seek out the *resources* needed to face any situation and confront those leaders who suggest that under-resourcing carries no risk. And remember: others within the organization carry the *Alarm P-Factors*, signaling to you, as the leader when danger or risk is present. Leaders must listen to these alarms when sounded by workers and respond correctly. Ignoring alarms can cause grave danger to the "hive."

The Colony Culture: A strong *colony culture* of collaboration, cooperation, and trust that happens uniformly and automatically at every place within the organization; a belief that being "in colony" will produce something exceptional, far greater than doing it alone. The beehive honeycomb pattern exemplifies this concept of being interdependent and united.

The Front Porch Philosophy, CAMP, and PRR: A way of looking at responsibility and accountability as a behavior that every employee accepts as they cross the "porch" to their organization. Based on the *CAMP* method of motivation—*Competence, Autonomy, Meaningfulness, and Progress*—employees make a commitment to self-discipline and self-direction. Leadership can use the *Prompt-Response-Reward Method* to build the passion and yearning to repeat responsible behaviors.

The Bee-2-Bee Waggle Dance and BUZZ: Bees have achieved a spontaneous and constant form of communication. Leaders can learn from the bees the value of defining their own *waggle dance* of communication as leaders and spread the *waggle dance* philosophy of communication throughout the organization, creating a unique and organic *BUZZ*.

The Perfect Product Honey Stream: Bees only know to make a Perfect Product. Their honey stream can contract and expand dramatically to meet the honey production needs of the hive in the short time between spring and summer. The rhythm of the honey flow—or perfect product—is known to every bee. Leaders today must be immersed in the flow of work in their own organizations, rather than observing from a removed position. Great leaders put themselves at the center of the organization and move openly amongst the workforce. They identify challenges, bottlenecks, and constraints and work with staff to address them every day.

Protect the Hive and Leaving the Post: Too often there are so many internal battles within organizations that no one is even watching for real risks—robbers—outside the hive. Leaders can learn to respond to those risks with the 4 Rs of *Research, Report, Respond, and Recover,* making sure not to react until the research confirms a problem and devoting time during recovery to surface, discuss and evaluate lessons learned. To make the *4Rs* work there must be a *leaving the post* mentality present that will protect against silo thinking and division.

◄ ►

When you have completed this book, we hope you will be reminded of the leadership lessons provided to Zync whenever you see a bee at work on a flower, or taste their perfect product—honey—in your cup of tea.

The End.

Authors' Bio

Deborah Mackin: Author of three best-selling teaming books, including *The Team-Building Tool Kit: Second Edition*, Mackin is an international business consultant, leadership coach, and workforce development trainer with over twenty-eight years of experience. Having worked alongside executives, leaders, and managers in some of the world's most prestigious companies, including Coca-Cola, Alcoa, Delta Faucet, the US Navy, and Sanofi Pasteur, Mackin is a veteran when it comes to what works in the business world today.

Matthew Harrington: Son and business partner with Deborah Mackin, Harrington is seen as a subject matter expert on social media, social learning, the Millennial generation, and new forms of leadership within the workplace. Harrington is quickly becoming a leading strategist working with organizations to help usher in a new era of leadership excellence.

Notes:

Deborah Mackin and Matthew Harrington are business partners at The New Directions Group, an innovative leadership, training and workforce development firm located in southern Vermont since 1984. The New Directions Group specializes in helping organizations get the most out of their people by raising the bar and inspiring leadership potential. Partnering with organizations to build a people-centered, high-engagement workplace, The New Directions Group provides services in facilitation management, employee training and development, staff and customer surveying, leadership and executive coaching, and organizational strategy and assessment. Some of their recent clients include Coca-Cola, Sanofi Pasteur, Alcoa, Bechtel Marine Propulsion, Ellis Medicine, and CAP COM Federal Credit Union. To Learn more visit www.NewDirectionsConsulting.com.

Made in the USA
Las Vegas, NV
20 April 2021